Copyright © 2019 Rocío Carlos
All rights reserved.
Typesetting by Janice Lee
Cover Art by Ana Chaidez
Cover Design by Esa Grigsby
Copyediting by Gabriela Torres Olivares (Spanish)
and Esa Grigsby (English)
ISBN 978-1-948700-16-0

THE ACCOMPLICES:
A #RECURRENT Book

theaccomplices.org

THE ACCOMPLICES

(the other house)

by Rocío Carlos

map/ legend

*

sin brújula, peregrina, says my father/ called wolf by my mother, a boy from the fading photograph. little match, he says, walk ahead. you who are young/ save our place. hide the key under your tongues, lizard, (he says)

how you learn the way, without speaking. your legs begin breaking. your spine curving. your voice changing from song to low growl.

(this is topography)

/

how could I know about fire/ how could you have warned me (and memory?)

this is how we died:

i went ahead into the woods and grew wild

                    i called the trees by name

my father the wolf fed me the names for this purpose

                    (i sewed them here, into my mouth)

*

what they don't tell you about raising your children in a foreign place/ is that they will be foreign too/ foreign to

points of/ departure

*mother's cathedral emptied out by officers. she returned with
a bowed head and a hand vacant of her heirloom/ mother,
you will soon orphan me/ how could you have given me
something the marauders would want*

(eldest/ you still have your body)

*nobody said this of course/ the body is an embarrassment/
what good is a thing so badly made that it breaks in the time
it takes to grow a daughter up to nothing*

*

mother
how many lovers I will have
I am not embarrassed
but I will not tell you because my body
is a language you never learned

                        but **your** body was my first language

take this body
let us   covenant

i was so young then

*

eldest, I will bead you white gowns full of worry/ I will take you to temple and teach you the singing of that other country (no hell to go to)/ but you will walk crooked, clumsy/ you will bruise like fruit/ I am sorry/ I must save some gifts for the one who comes after you...

/

(the last thing i remembered was the word fruit)

because I heard you coming, I abandoned my lessons
I stepped away, into some wild place

(nacimiento)

that place of damp earth/ do you remember it/ i stole a handful of it to eat slowly/ to remember you before i knew you/ *and you are?*

*

rivers are born and grow up in your childhood
you fashion, then, a guardian of the waters/
your parents bring you north
to a dry place, a place of dying

(and fires)

but i was waiting here for you/ with a forked tongue
and your name was already written on my skin

call me that again, that word

father (black and a wolf and a wild reed besides),

                    i fell into the thorns and bit through my tongue.

i drowned in a pool.
my legs are always bruised.
my skin does not age.
          it is a fresh page every day.
the names are written there daily.
i am saving a place for when you come, a shelter made of names, of my skin.

remember me, the darker one? the one with the temper and birthmark like him (and her? was i ever like her?)

*

am I separate from them, my family?
am I separate from the forest?
and my tongue, is it not forked as a river?

north, like the nile
follow the sound of your name

(howl)

there is a clearing/ a doorway
so many metaphors for casually open legs
foreign my own hand to my body

(the hand of malediction/ making a key or legend/ or the
sign of the cross)

PROCENIUM/ signum crucis

Thrust:

(here) is your mother's hand gesturing

toward curtain and frame (some edge, some forever fall)

imagine: index finger pointing down

aquí está el infierno/ *no hell to go to*

thumb folded over tightly

aquí está mi abrazo/ this

in the name of names and not

that is to say un-names/ sin nombre

I gave you her name.

*

(here) is your father's song as compass/ compás

a way to keep time/ true north

empezar llorando/ acabar cantando (como quien dice)

and to say/ say this: cut a hollow in the frame

crush pomegranates where you wipe your feet

where you wipe your feet, both entry and limit

(the cliff/ the weight of eyelids)

behind you: bruised feet through a keyhole

before you, open mouths and folded hands

a torn screen, swinging doors

y dice así:

autobiography of a scar

*

(sometimes when you are washing your hair, this happens)
you condition your hair/ to go see your mother/ you
make it soft and shiny so she remembers you/ when
you were four years old. your mother
creator and destroyer
attends/ says
where are you my eldest/
i made you of coffee bean and milk/ i named you after the sea spray/
after the madonna of a dark people
in a white savanna/ i carried you
across the desert,
flake of snow/ on the map
of my body/ be counted.
i (eldest) *gave you* (eldest)/ *the hands of*
maura (eldest)/ *after she lost*
the finger of malediction/ (or was it the other thing/the other hand).
with them you traced the scars that range
across mother's pale body/when you asked if they were your
doing the only answer was ever yes.
mother summons and your/ mouth looses the wicked phrase/
put there by marauders

(mande usted).

extraño

how strange is missing you when you are here

the strangeness of missing something/ how foreign a body

as bodies beget bodies

how neatly we fit into each other/ how your fingers are just more of me

cognates in word and deed:

my blood and flesh weaving in some northern place you couldn't know:

stranger.

*

you were born in the far away/ I didn't know you then

you spoke a foreign tongue called *mother*

do you miss your mother/ or the idea of her

memory/ language

conflating the two tongues
(how foreign, spoken language)
i pointed at a bird of prey and said *égola*
my father said only yes and led me away
the word for dam is presa. the word for prisoner is presa.
the word for prey is presa. the word for cursing is damn. the
word for knowing is damn.

(we won't even talk about garras we won't even talk)

ships: niña/ pinta/ santa maría

en este cuento/ yo todavía no nacía/ no era ni tierra ni astro

érase una vez, dijiste me dijiste, había una brújula

in the dark

i learned:

there are many darknesses

mother pierced my ears as soon as i was old enough to weep. when she saw that i did not cry, she threaded my body with gold. she laid needle and thread close to my fingers. guardian, she says. you keep us hidden. you are bridge and water. little frost, lay your long body in the wilderness.

on fire(s)

a burning bird was my teacher/ what did i know, innocent of a language/ the caged rooster in the courtyard with feathers like something immolated/ snapped at my hand and aimed for my eyes/

this is how i was made, near the sea or near the cotton fields. or in a mother-in-law's adobe house, or a borrowed room. or under the southern star, or at first light. long and willowy with an angry look. better to look like a tree.

(october/ oh santa ana wind/ i see you coming for my body)

this came with some thirst
learning the names of trees in that other tongue,
a place to wait for you in slumber

(i dreamed i forgot us and was new as clay
a mouth mouthing in the direction of rain)

mouths, like rivers, run dry.

the little boy across the street, his house is on fire/ my father runs into the house even as smoke wilts the jacaranda/ it was a mattress i think.

my father's father runs into the house even as the smoke wilts the cotton/ it was a girl/

///

on past tense of being/

(if) we never pronounce the word

(where does that sound wait to be said/ where does it wait forever)

*

was she or wasn't she

old enough to know the word   fuego/ lumbre

old enough to be afraid

old enough to know the hand that

reached for her in the smoke meant to save her

old enough to remember me

*

was/ were:

we were little, both of us looking across time

at each other except i got big you never got big

what did you get instead (you got left)

when i learned your secret name what i learned was

the future will be imperfect

even as you grew up, the Colorado was first there
(everything was there—the wild valley
between the desert and the sea)
and then not there at all/
an ancient álamo,
the wells that beg for water: all words to forget

*

the little girl too?
(my first cradle, that bridge away from you and toward her)

sometimes you struggle to remember the other language
river reed, the language you pressed on my hand with your hand
those afternoon walks in a gray world
you forget how to speak except to tell me
this is how you lose a world

tongues bite/ i bite my tongue/ i cannot ask about her*

(like all of my life/ like everything else, this is a lie)

when fires come you are a fawn's mother and then you are
the fawn/ (innocent of language) you realize the theft of the
body/ the gift of the body

when those boys in the stairwell tried to take away your body/
you gave your curse to them (language: a fist and long leg)

when your mother lied to you about the translation of
taking away a body, by instinct you already knew the danger
of saying what was true

and what is true?
what i said, or what my body said?
                           (which one is me/ which one is you)

language: a flaming bird

i am laid down on a blanket in the grass to learn a wilderness

this is more important than street names

i am trucha before i can walk

in obedience, my brow becomes a valley/

my mother sews me with bright veins

my father hides a compass under my tongue

this is the map of our steps

look in a mirror to find your way home

but while i was away/ a drought came

maldición: a handed curse, desire. if i am the map/ how could you not find me

sequia/ ausencia

those sundays the record player said to me to forget it.
i listened for my mother's anger or my father's hangover:
the sound of church bells.
or the smell of oil frying, my father's hair oil too,
floral and chemical together. the record player translated.

(here was the future's lesson)

tell lies, it directed me again and again.
tell them you came from some strange land without suffering,
that you do not know sorrow, because you have never loved.

you, your language being made and unmade.
your name being given and taken.
your legs steadying and then kicked out from under you.

(where I am going, i will speak of your love as a golden dream)

(the lost)

afraid of sorcery,
the son of the augur and haruspex
drew a map of the known world

beware my girl, the cucuy and chamuco/ *trucha*

(this was its own magic)

your mother, flower and daughter of the flower-eater
gave you the instrument of war,
made a language with her hands/ something else for you to lose

you asked the lady with the vest to find your mother/ how easily you lost her

you still have a body, after all
you still have the compass

smoke and its sources

you found the forest, little match
the names told you they were there
(in the name of names, make that sign)

your temper a north star—
this is how you will be found,
wild and full of the language of trees in a place of drought

don't go away- i long for you/ i love the longing for you/

a map with the legend missing:
this is my body, useless with desire
and death? where is that place

                                             (and what border)

where you learn my name and you say it to me
(tell me again)

seven years old and accustomed to making maps
i named the places hidden from me
(you still have your body, eldest)
words came untucked from my tongues

*

what wanting is when you are raised in drought/
a poverty of its own
*we are so quiet and so clean we are so silent we are not even
      here*

foreign/ language

early you learn the story:
a desperate mother drowns her own children
and proceed with caution: living, that is.
but you were born under the sign of the crab
como quien dice, it was a role you were born to play

*

those years of cold and rain followed you through a desert
even as you were only a twinkle in the shadow of a border wall
you hold your breath in case of smoke because there is a
story for that too

points of light*

stone or plank/ that sinking feeling
when you are seven years old
in the Parras' pool
the scales of light shimmering above you/ below you
just who is speaking now/ just who is spoken to
and what beast's tentacle wraps around your long thin arm.
(I was practicing speaking a language
my mother didn't know/ I was singing
a song in your animal tongue)

*
*after, the adults laughing and toasting tell you you are fine/
you are just fine. you don't wear glasses yet, but the dry
world is the same as under the water. perhaps this is why you
weren't certain yet that you were drowning*

a translation of sorrows:

four in the morning fog.
dew/ your mother's word for the dampness of you

standing next to mother
to answer men and women
who stamp forms

firstborn. translate
*residency   *   alien   *   proof*

(¿y tu hermana?)

your mother's white body standing tall and staring the strangers in the face when you speak good English (when did you learn English, exactly? when did the words sneak into your tongue? and did you surprise yourself?)

lines in a stairwell where you twist your hands. your name the dew. walking through the body of yourself.

what the teacher said after, when your mother spoke through a neighbor's mouth: Rocío is a very pretty little girl.

not sunsets but fires
that half turn toward the dying
is a walk into auntie's tiny embrace
remember me/ your twin's firstborn (you say to the mirror)

what remembering does to a body: *an invented history*

or is it inventory
(how you screw words into each other to make a new word):

your legs are breaking and making themselves again
your wrists cannot take the weight of your hands
and your lungs remember both smoke and water
you can't see
your mouth is always bleeding
and that other place
well, it is teething too.

guardian,
in this way you became what you are
both memory and premonition

the darkest of us even in the north
your name a drop of blood or was it water
something fine and beautiful to hear

*

where is my country/ it is a body/ it is your body/ this song *howling* is the sound/ of your name/ in my father's country/ the morning song/ and the song of the flood/ and drought/ and the sunset song/ and the song of the cold/ was that clipped yelp and long whine/ was you in flight/ was the song of your mouth   *howling*   the sound of my name

      we gathered our littles and ran to the end of our block
      we were gathered we were blocked

you were once smallest/ you were once only
a wild thing and protection from the wild. mother sewed
your skirts with scales/ father handed you a blade with a
mother of pearl blade to remember your mother with

we smelled rain coming and headed toward the river. we
invented burials and mourning.
      we were only children.
      we found the dead god and shielded our littles' eyes
      we gathered oleander and did not eat it.

in a thick fog you rose with the morning star
you went ahead into the wilderness/ they didn't see you
take your sister tightly by the wrist/

someone who died (someone to die for)
                                                a secular song sings
poor thing/ do you have a sister

on haunted houses/ *mother*

here you are untucked from a bed of pearls and ferried across the belly of a dry sea. here is a body, the bed of pearls. here is language, little pearl. it is also a pearl.

and you, pearl of occident?

i was made in the place where the arroyo is born. i ended drought by looking up. i crossed the desert and unlearned speech. i gave you the instrument of war, eldest.

you still have your body/

house that wants to be haunted

you open your mouth and let language enter

at rest and in motion (what good is a body)

when i was four i misplaced my mother's hand
a lady in a vest told me in wayward spanish
to speak my mother's name, a word i had not learned

learning the language of movement/ that I am compass and sailor/ that I am pulled away and toward some equatorial kiss/ the lift of my long arms toward some firmament (that we have a separate word for firmament)/ a language sewn into me/ I was knitted together that year you crossed the sea

*

when i was eight years old, i approached a southern border alone.

the tape rolling backward/ a daughter in reverse
east instead of west, south instead of north
I squatted over a spider's nest in the sand
I pretended to sleep at the checkpoints
a dog hid under my legs
and we drove over unfinished roads
I sat up and looked out at the dark,
the darknesses under riverless bridges
I was delivered at night to my mother's mother's house
(who was pregnant with me even as she knitted together a mother for me)
in reverse, my tongue reaching for memory of a language I learned first
so dark-skinned and from the north, as if the north should bleach me
do you really speak english, my cousins asked
we wore white eyelet and chased each other in the cotton fields:

                it was communion season/ it was may.

covenants

that morning i hollered for my mother in english
she said to me don't tell your father
and drove me to school late
a document written by my body appeared
in a language i learned
when i fell asleep in my porta-bebe
with my new arracadas caught on my sweater/ quietly,
that language seeped into the fibers
of my homemade sweater and my hair
and visited my tongue again when i fell
 into doña amparo's roses
or when i slipped on my roller skates
or when i lost teeth to so many invisible mice—
the language of an arrangement,
a contract i have not upheld

when words fail/ ghosts appear
my gender feels like my childlessness
(I call the name and no one comes)

the forest murmurs: what a quiet world after all

(a secular song)

the song of that other wilderness
my body, that tower of noise
so many names/ tongues
we ended a world every time
writing
        (what the body is for)
a document of longing

what (is the body) for

in a bed of pearls I sew a spell:
my mother the seamstress/ my father the farmer
plunging and lifting the instrument of survival (cervical)
in my flesh that autumn/ how greedy I was
there could be no one after me to tell the tale

*

*i wrote your name in the soft bed of my embrace/ in that
language we never shared but looked at together/ the
flourishes of a placemat border that time we spilled our
waters reaching for each other*

*the distance is what makes us, is it not: the always wanting
and glancing and brushing
and always knowing the end and then the next beginning/
the fine arrangement of the universe.*

*

and what is home even
in a body when that body
is snatched/ is bounced from map
to map/ to be a map

cerca

a sign (rótulo, mother calls it) tells you where you are: a place the size of your suffering

threshold/ and no place to knock   when you make a
fist, you strike yourself   the place the size of your fist
(the size of your suffering) is a mirror   in your mother's
purse that you reach for in long lines   waiting for ways to
translate the word   *entry*

little match,
how you closed the door
on the rest of the house
and lit a candle in the home
of a father frightened by fire

and learned the word for the unthinkable
how the wreaths of smoke became a language
you stumbled toward on those bad legs
wreathed in veins (how like smoke)
like someone running from a fire

shriven

*

how I love this burning/ here/ bless me here/
and bless all those who have blessed me before you/

*

as if it was not work to bring about destruction (a bonfire of vanities)/
in your navel in the twin marks on your lips/ the mirror says, that's where it is/ you turn away in time to hear the song of mourning, to hear hands wringing:

cartographer/ map the body swollen knees the bones and fine hands the path to the door the way home to a longing and so many broken chopsticks/ a crumbling mountain, so much rain

(which flood)

(joy)

stubborn door, this skin
and burial in this body sounds of laughter and breaking and instruments the body as instrument the line of a childhood a turning away or running away/ *wilderness*/ starting from a home to a world/ a life the ocean for the first time

(the first time the tide lapped at my ankles I wept with shame/ I apologize mother this is my body/ my father held my hand and laughed at the water).

while you are away/ maps change shape
*(how want **wants**)*
dizzy with survival
you imagined a future,

a horizon in close proximity

here is a broken body/ there is a bruised wilderness/ the
body in a wilderness making new an autumn a time of sleep
and graying

I picked glass from the soil to protect my family
I nursed a sore paw
the calico follows me wherever I go/
she is not afraid of wolves

*

fever when it comes is a house on fire is the unrelenting
rain far from the body that suffers cold I saw you or the
mirage of you or was it your shadow or did I dream you/ I
had a little aunt who was only ash and she never answers
when I call (arrow catcher, here come ashes)

what remembering does to a body. i ask my ghosts/
are you satisfied?

*

the roughness of fingers which point and wave/ the history of forgetting (this reminds me of)

But there are fires to forget but we can't forget even when we don't remember (I remember her/ my color, my scowl the lost twin soul) they say the old dragon drank to forget her. I think it was to remember. A tired and sad dragon, he was cruel except to me. His laughter made the doves trill away from the palms. He lifted me onto the red filly. He told me she was mine and I named her Golondrina, after the birds that never stay.

you carry the place/ the death/ where is a place not crooked not covered in dust left by a terrible night left by those wonderful nights and the night of loss too and the nights of laughter

(que no le temo a la muerte)

burn/break/live
or not
some cell in your body deciding what to do what comes next and the atoms of the universe arrange themselves in such a way to let you pass.
what the ocean is/ what names map/ what use is the body that can be broken/ or taken/ that just fades away.

I make viscous nests and tear them down
I fill my mouth with blood and say your name

(what prayers are)

*

Paterfamilias

(lent/body of)
a shadow
a bone   its marrow
a hand/ a body
under another's hand and care
a tiny death (mine)
I wait for a sun
I want to be
your first place
that place of
snow marked
by your breath
the mystery of
all of the leaving naming and the longing
and I want it to be my name my song
and I am not okay and can't say the words
across the plains and trees

(in march there is death and longing and the
month of march does not belong to me)

(and death?)

death comes to your bedside before they know they should call a doctor. death is turned away by your mother's witchcraft—

you learned to breathe south somewhere

death comes to your play date/ swims with you and then/ only she is swimming. death is turned away by your friend's father's long arm, fishing you limp out of the pool.

death comes for the paterfamilias. you are man of the house now. and second witch. three witches turn away death. youngest chants the call. mother lights the candle she kept from her mother's wake/ in this way/ you too call death by name.

imagine this spell

in writing, imagine
this summoning, imagine
my voice, rings of smoke
(a key turning in the dark)

how you enter this home of my wilderness
without wiping your feet

imagine my bones, cast
as stones in pine clearings
imagine you writing the spell
(begin on my inner right thigh/
finish on my lower lip)

lay down your language, your breath
imagine your matted coat here
where we lose everything but our touch

i am learning a voice to call you with. i am learning to cast a shadow that is a door for you to crawl through that last time. i will say your name. i have spelled it with the bones of my clavicle.

how to say oleander:

in translation/ some sorrow
is more mine to give

(little stranger) you came from so far away

so here, take this body and eat it
it is my sorrow
(it is mine to give)

i looked at the brick courtyard and thought i saw the old priest from my home parish dressed in black/ with white hair; he was smiling/ he was saying something with his hands. it sounded like my name, which is not my name at all/ i borrowed it from the other country/ i dressed myself in the damp mist to be hidden from the drought's teeth/ until the time you come

femmes maisons

how time stops in floods and abductions how a house in lavender fields speaks a language my mother tucked away for me to find dressed in white eyelet: house-ness or home-ness

I made you in my mouth (the word made flesh) I made you to live inside of damp/ viscous tethers as claws come to a point/ little alpha/ anonymous/ a cast away inside me

(a place for a heart-beat to live)

time in suspension,

as if asleep in thick syrup, my mother teaches me to cast spells

*

how a body tolerates all this longing/ the emptiness of sea
horses/ uncoiled and unbridled/ where tides tug
(a house wanting to be haunted)
bower-bird's daughter
what is reason
when in november the roads burn
donde aterrizas también hay mar y aquí sólo panteones
all i have is a clean floor and a clean house big and empty

*late in the morning you ask me to look at something on your
body, the way people together for a long time do.*

nido

if i see the word vientre one more time...
(haunted)

*

punch through that finely-wrought tissue
when i miss you i ovulate— i am the bower-bird's daughter:
i find and gather thread and colored glass
i get up early and sweep until my bare feet don't pick up any crumbs
i go outside and count the dying trees/ the world is ending and you are so far away

*

i'm going to set this house on fire and stand on the roof
guiding the smoke stacks the plumes of smoke so that from
where you are you can hear one of them saying my name

the full moon of august trickling down my thigh (how many poems have I written with something leaking out of me, smeared on my legs)

The unpicked figs. My mother returns from her mother's lap and mantle, unscathed. What it is to have a mother that eats her young. How each woman is three women at once when she is carrying a woman. How in my grandmother my body was already absent. Where did you go, eldest, where have you been? How we have the same voice. Orphaned, the two in front of me turn back and let down their rebozos. My mother is a pause in a dark sentence. From Maura to me the words are olive-colored. Our eyes wide but sunken, ringed in purple pigment. Fruit shrivels on trees while I wait.

(all houses have ghosts, don't they)

ajeno

oh stranger/ little stranger/ as in foreign as of not of me/ how could i not know you and still build you from thoughts and then tissue/ how could i sit next to my mother and not be seen by her/ both of us far from our mothers/ both of us good at making ghosts/

*(one day when your wife means to call you husband
she will call you wolf instead)*

*

your eldest huddled you beside a fire/ your song kept the wolves away

you were just a boy, ankle deep in prawns in the desert fields/ during the watering time/ a dying river nearby wailed for daughters

a melancholy child/ inside you was already the memory of me

(having crossed so many rivers)
you become accustomed
to approaching gates and their keepers

there was always/ this walk to the north/ inside us
and I have brought you from the place
where the river dried up and the fire swallowed our family
you, with the good language/ and the bad temper
all I can give you is permission to guard the ruins of a
forgotten place

how (like pearls) bridges crumble
a forest rises from the ruins
waiting for that name,
you speak that spell sewed deep in your throat

danse oriental/ women dancing

here is a garment of other tongues by other hands
what east means in a desert in a place of veils. your mother/
pearl of occident/ who covered and showed you to cover
did not teach you that word in the thickness of your
thighs/ which you found in a western tongue
THUNDER a cousin said, to make you cry

harnesser of storms stays veiled with a blade in hand
(que en cielo fuiste estrella)
and finds the word for mother
in your fingerprint a bruise the size of the desert
you make that language/
(men look on)

how finishing

is in the act of beginning.
how my cells faded
even hours after i was begun
and how i was begun
as an end to your long walk/

                                        dear god

I love this burn in my throat

(but) death:

words gather in grief
this page too
your hand touching it
your tongue holding my name
you are gathered by me
you are spoken into being by me
(call me *guardian*)

(commit this sacrament)

and burial and burial and burial a song again a lingering
and forming how like a life how the body becomes and then
disappears

*mother who gives permission to cry who makes the rain and
drought*
mountains crumble so that forests can rise under the feet
of wolves
(something about peaches and moons/ a potted mint and
portraiture)
and what things quake, a limb, a lip, the continent with my
desire for your trembling and my body as this wilderness
what trembling and then stillness
old as wolves I want to hold your face my
(sparrow the kind of bird who keeps secrets)

*my grandfather who called me by my saint's name trembled
and one by one the long cells of his muscle tissue became a
blanket of sleep and he couldn't say any of my names, not
even call me eldest.*

passeri aves

flight and solitude cloaked/ *deciduous*
(where desire is tucked for safe keeping)
where you give me small public kisses
(a wildness of matted wet fur, or salt on ice)
tell me again what you said to the others.

yes

yes

yes

you

you

you

(your name)

(your name)

(your name)

your skin

your skin

your skin

how to dance to remember

                              (this is a language I speak)/

and how to forget the way back

a pivot, a doorway

(how your body went bad and broke, how we put you back together)

in a museum, tulle wings hang from the ceiling

i tell you I dance/ *i used to dance*

like this, like a family in flight, like the migration of birds *black and*   blue (beard)/ silent except for the sound of/ wind thrashing past trees/ my neck a sapling in January/ standing up to the rush of air/ waiting for death/ before it realizes it is simply your breath/ the wild language of saying my name.

(a)flame/ a body on fire

how fevers come *in spoken spells*

speak, guardian, the name that frees us

that glows in your mouth as pearls glow in the mouths of mothers

it is so cold here, where wolves sing

my mother wore azahares in her desert marriage/ i crush citrus leaves and hold my palm to your mouth/ the difference being only veils/ and thirst

(a difference between a grave and a marriage bed)

*

i made a bed of crushed leaves/ that year you crossed some desert or some sea

hostia:

my body is the body that comes between bodies
                                                                                       howling
my body is between you and snows
                                                                                        howling
my body is the door and lock
                                                                                        howling
and here my body parts the forest open
howling
and is a nest of leaves and the roar of waves
                                                                                        howling

my body is the new year

what archive here/ here is a fossil,
a walk in the rain/ to avoid clichés, do
not look nature in the eye (the storm
that is) here comes your mother's voice
the light reaching for you a mother's
hand coming for you the clap and roar
of her, calling your name *morning*

entre comillas

así vivimos/ apenitas viviendo/
mi aliento: costal de gatos
esta niña se va a morir/ decía mi tía
                                                   pero viví, así
en los paréntesis y asteriscos de una vida
tus manos, mamá, planchando toallitas
y untándome vaporú en el pecho

me tenías prestada de un almacén de deseos
pero me criaste/ ajena
al lenguaje que sería mío primero y tuyo después
así que me enseñaste mi primer idioma, el anhelo

foreign from my maker/ except for our hands. do you see, my love: the hand of malediction

(I cursed for the first time by making a fist)

we sit across from each other and compare hands. and here, this mark/ that knob/ or gesture

(we point together to make the lights come on and off and laugh/ we are witches!)

we sew worry into our bodies and mouths

(our pretty shared hands) wrung as bells.

I grew long fingers unfit for rings/ I made a compass's needle of my body

my thin wrists: these are for housing your sorrows

(you never kiss my wrists)

I want the bad word in your mouth/ that word for despair

(I already know it)

februaries/ it never stops raining/ we brace for the spring and it's scythe/ we ride trains to festivals and watch parades/

how in crowds i imagine being lost from and finding you/ how many crowds were we in together before we met?/ how many times humming the same song/ speaking the same mother tongue of skin/ i touch as many strangers as i can in case one of them is a past or future you...

finding some road home I pass under bridges and nod to guardians there/ my mother is from the place of waters/ she made me a dragon as well

*

save this/ me:

it was only a movie/ we were so young
that day in the desert/ the door-less frame

(you turn knobs/ you look up as knobs turn)

hands at work/ pull on this bad knee and ankle
joints bandaged up and braided together
tell the crows/ tell them what/
that/ that well-worn shirt/
belongs to me

past you/ future you

our hands dusted in chalk in classrooms and our knees stained by grass/ that photosynthetic smell/ that damp soil smell/ I want you on forest floors/ I want you on blacktop city lots/ or running from a night to our home covered in animal hair/ remember the running to our mothers as the light changed/ except only I have always run to my mother, every time/ you are wild/ and stay out without permission or explanation/ no matter: we are both exactly our mothers' sorrows and their deepest worry/ we are both the children that don't come when called/

I summoned you with the compass of my body/ our tribes a sea of foreheads facing north/ you came as the cold was thawing/ unaccustomed, we crushed citrus leaves and hoped for floods/ we mistook red clay for good soil/ and watched trees struggle in the cold/ I was always the body that suffered cold/ I grew a silver coat over this body/ how did we live/ we made houses of steam/ in order to live

comunión

on some brink
your face, the darkness
with empty hands
(this house is always burning)

where cotton fields steam with song
not far from where fires curl fields
we wear white in surrender to the sacrament
that requires death in exchange for life/ fasting
except for orange blossoms:

here the other country where my sorrows are sown

where language is made by hands

on kissing:
only strangers/ ajeno
kissing on the mouth as if we could transmit *hunger*
all of my lovers blessing my stomach at once for your sake
so that you could be the one who finds the compass's needle
the one who sees home written in the language of longing
my first language and yours too

temblor

the song of me building a language
little, do you hear?
i stole the song from the place of waters
it's in the music box next to my bed
(for when the candle runs out)

if I say it with dirt in my mouth
will you hear/ our mother's song
splitting floor open

remember your gifts
the language of sorrow
a never ending thirst.

when you long for me
does it sound like the roar of waves
when i long for you
it sounds like the washing machine
tumbling our sheets free of animal

innocence is uncrossed line, after all

how I let you cross the threshold of my home
and in some dark break some seal
old and brittle but real as words as okay and yes
and the words I didn't say*
and how the cold was colder after that
and I felt fearless, *I felt like women who are not afraid of men.*

what you miss is my body
(as map and compass)
the body as a document
here write your memories
the record player instructed   *write the names to forget them*

holding me—

what's there, a name
for you to recognize in some future

(none of us spoke this language/ my parents don't speak it anymore) mornings we find the fog heavy in some wilderness. *oh wild world*. this is my body/ (take this all of you)

mother/ the language you do not speak is the language of me reaching for her/ for all of them

what is the language for a house that burns/ that doesn't burn
where is a house not haunted
and a body not made for breaking

i have grown a forest from the words
left over from the translations of our sorrows
my body the map of drought
your name the song in my throat

waiting for that last bridge on fire to shudder open a world

what was it you wanted to say about my face as we leaned sideways against the wall in the house of swirling ghosts. no shortage of haunting or smoke/ here is smoke but no fire (just looking for words and not finding them)

(((and then there is the beacon   and then there is
homecoming)))

this is how you began (in the other house)

father heals in coats of pain
ghosts linger in corridors
a son's bones (the light/ the storm/ the storm's harnesser)

that sleep hammer/ how you hold it
and I let you how I let you/ so that we have matching wounds
learning right/ wrong

I put my body between my mother and my sister's body/ she never missed I didn't let her miss. once, younger, stupid, I ducked or ran from her and I was sorry

what names float the ghost name
the girl who won't come when called
except that I have no name to call her
I use smoke as signals the way my mother does with me
(can a house be built can a house be moved   what is *there*)
there is
there is
(disappearing people)

—breaking as waves as glass slippers/ what makers demand
what salt is: protection against the works of others
or misfortune/
what is language but tripwire/ or a bridge
from far away sisters wave to us
the hand that holds your name like longing/ when
I put my teeth together to say your first syllable my mouth
waters with sorrow

*

the places where you are from are always
on fire this city or that country or this body
(what if I told you this city of yours is my body
I have mapped it in bridges and train tracks)

el nombre de la estación *verano*
el nombre de quién/ de cuál canción

and what are anchors? cement? names? gods?

ghosts: yellow the color of everything but the sun even as it
dies in a place so far from where you were
born/ here in the north your body holds blame

the body/ of me
which you conjured
and brought forth in some sleep

                                                  (it has been such a long night)

ROCÍO CARLOS attends from the land of the chaparral. Born and raised in Los Ángeles, she is widely acknowledged to have zero short term memory but know the names of trees. Her other books include *Attendance* (The Operating System) and *A Universal History of Infamy: Those of This America* (LACMA/Golden Spike Press). She was selected as a 2003 Pen Center "Emerging Voices" fellow. She collaborates as a partner at Wirecutter Collective and is a teacher of the language arts. Her favorite trees are the olmo (elm) and aliso (sycamore).

OFFICIAL

THE **ACCOMPLICES**

GET OUT OF JAIL
* VOUCHER *

- -

Tear this out.
Skip that social event.
It's okay.
You don't have to go if you don't want to. Pick up
the book you just bought. Open to the first page.
You'll thank us by the third paragraph.

If friends ask why you were a no-show, show them
this voucher.
You'll be fine.

- -

We're thriving.

CPSIA information can be obtained
at www.ICGtesting.com
Printed in the USA
FSHW010553150219
55694FS